ABDO Publishing Company

BUGS!
Cockroaches

Kristin Petrie

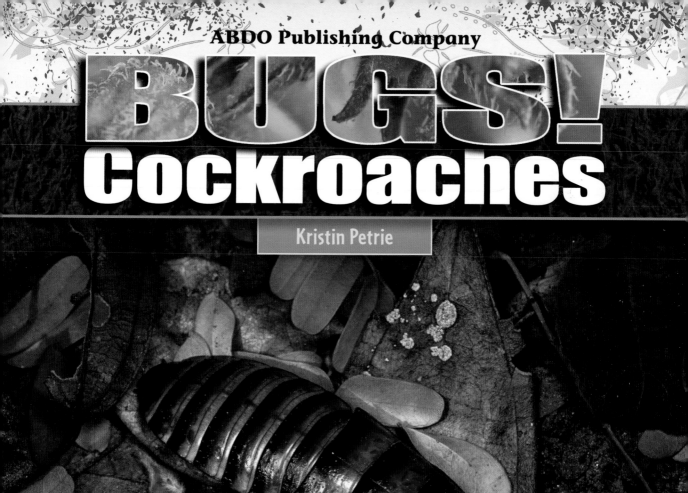

visit us at
www.abdopublishing.com

Published by ABDO Publishing Company, 8000 West 78th Street, Edina, Minnesota 55439.
Copyright © 2009 by Abdo Consulting Group, Inc. International copyrights reserved in all
countries. No part of this book may be reproduced in any form without written permission from the
publisher. The Checkerboard Library™ is a trademark and logo of ABDO Publishing Company.

Printed in the United States.

Cover Photo: Getty Images
Interior Photos: AP Images pp. 5, 29; Brian Jorg/CritterZone.com p. 9;
    Daniel R. Suiter/Bugwood.org p. 21; Dennis Sheridan/CritterZone.com pp. 15, 19, 28;
    Getty Images pp. 1, 11, 22; Glenn McCrea/CritterZone.com p. 7; iStockphoto pp. 17, 24, 27;
    Peter Arnold p. 20; Photo Researchers pp. 12-13, 23, 25; R. Martyniak/University of Florida
    p. 16; R.W. Baldwin/University of Florida pp. 16, 17

Series Coordinator: BreAnn Rumsch
Editors: Megan M. Gunderson, BreAnn Rumsch
Art Direction & Cover Design: Neil Klinepier

Library of Congress Cataloging-in-Publication Data

Petrie, Kristin, 1970-
  Cockroaches / Kristin Petrie.
      p. cm. -- (Bugs!)
  Includes index.
  ISBN 978-1-60453-066-7
  1. Cockroaches--Juvenile literature. I. Title.

  QL505.5.P48 2008
  595.7'28--dc22

                          2008004789

Contents

Cool Cockroaches

The sight of a cockroach makes different people do different things. Some wrinkle their nose in disgust. Others scream and run in the other direction. Many grab the nearest shoe to stop it dead.

There are many reasons for these reactions. Cockroaches have creepy antennae and hairy legs. They are also hard to catch! Cockroaches always seem to know when to run. Even if you catch one, their tough armor makes them hard to squash.

Cockroaches also love to be in the places where you don't want them. This includes your kitchen sink, your bathroom, and maybe even your bed! Even worse, they leave their droppings everywhere and have a stinky smell. Who wouldn't consider these bugs pests?

Believe it or not, some people enjoy cockroaches. They like the roach's helmet-shaped head, beady eyes, and fast legs. And, they think cockroaches make great pets. Do these cockroach fans know something that others do not?

Keep reading and you may become interested in roaches, too. Will you want one as a pet? Maybe not. However, you may not screech or run away the next time you see one.

Madagascar hissing cockroaches are not household pests. Instead, these bugs live on forest floors in groups called colonies.

What Are They?

Cockroaches are one of the oldest known insects. Some **entomologists** believe they have been on Earth for almost 400 million years! Back then, cockroaches were one of the first groups of flying insects.

Like all insects, cockroaches are from the class Insecta. Within this class, cockroaches belong to the order Dictyoptera and the **suborder** Blattaria.

The suborder Blattaria is further divided into two **superfamilies** and five families. These cockroaches have names such as wood cockroaches, giant cockroaches, and sand cockroaches. Altogether, there are nearly 4,000 cockroach species.

Each species of cockroach has a two-word name called a binomial. A binomial combines the genus with a descriptive name, or epithet. For example, a German cockroach's binomial is *Blattella germanica*.

THAT'S CLASSIFIED!

SCIENTISTS USE A METHOD CALLED SCIENTIFIC CLASSIFICATION TO SORT THE WORLD'S LIVING ORGANISMS INTO GROUPS. EIGHT GROUPS MAKE UP THE BASIC CLASSIFICATION SYSTEM. IN DESCENDING ORDER, THEY ARE DOMAIN, KINGDOM, PHYLUM, CLASS, ORDER, FAMILY, GENUS, AND SPECIES.

THE PHRASE "DEAR KING PHILIP, COME OUT FOR GOODNESS' SAKE!" MAY HELP YOU REMEMBER THIS ORDER. THE FIRST LETTER OF EACH WORD IS A CLUE FOR EACH GROUP.

DOMAIN IS THE MOST BASIC GROUP. SPECIES IS THE MOST SPECIFIC GROUP. MEMBERS OF A SPECIES SHARE COMMON CHARACTERISTICS. YET, THEY ARE DIFFERENT FROM ALL OTHER LIVING THINGS IN AT LEAST ONE WAY.

Body Parts

Like all insects, cockroaches have six legs, three body **segments**, and no bones. Instead of a skeleton inside its body, a cockroach has an exoskeleton made of chitin. This hard, shell-like substance covers the cockroach's entire body.

The exoskeleton has many functions. For example, it protects the roach's **organs** and keeps them in place. The exoskeleton also has an oily coating that prevents the cockroach from drying out.

Most cockroaches are dark brown to reddish brown in color. However, some species break the rules. For example, the Cuban banana cockroach has a lime green exoskeleton! This blends nicely into its leafy surroundings.

Cockroaches also come in many sizes. The smallest known cockroach is smaller than a sesame seed. Large species grow to about three inches (8 cm) long. The most well-known species include American cockroaches. These roaches are around one inch (3 cm) in length.

BUG BYTES

Cockroaches are extremely tough creatures. For example, a cockroach that has been frozen can fully recover if warmed up!

Cockroaches can flatten themselves to fit into cracks as thin as a dime. Their oily coating helps them squeeze into these tight hiding places.

A cockroach's three body **segments** are the head, the thorax, and the abdomen. The cockroach's head is covered by a hard shield called the pronotum.

Two long antennae stick out from under the pronotum. The antennae serve as the cockroach's strongest sense **organs**. They help it sense sounds and smells.

A cockroach has two compound eyes on its head. Each compound eye has around 2,000 lenses. This allows the roach to see movement in many directions at once! Some cockroach species have additional eyes called ocelli. These eyes detect light and dark.

Chewing mouthparts are found on the underside of a cockroach's head. These include mandibles, or upper jaws, and maxillae, or lower jaws. Two pairs of pinchers called palpi are also present. The palpi act like fingers. They hold and taste food while the jaws grind it into tiny pieces.

Behind the cockroach's head is the thorax. This body segment is the connecting point for two sets of wings. The forewings form a protective shield over the hind wings.

BUG BYTES

If a roach loses its head, it can continue to walk around. It may survive for a week before dying of thirst.

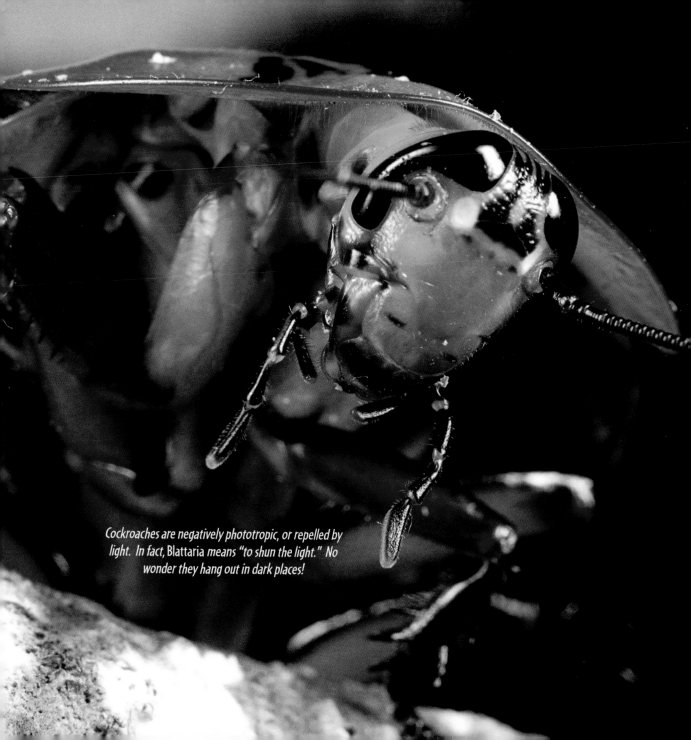

Cockroaches are negatively phototropic, or repelled by light. In fact, Blattaria means "to shun the light." No wonder they hang out in dark places!

To fly, a cockroach lifts its forewings to reveal the hind wings. The hind wings are lightweight and delicate. Some cockroach species have long wings. Others have short wings. Whatever their wing length, most cockroaches never fly at all.

The thorax is also the connecting point for three sets of jointed legs. Each leg ends with a clawed foot. In addition, the bottom of each foot is coated with a sticky surface. These features help the cockroach climb almost anywhere, including on your ceiling!

A COCKROACH'S BODY

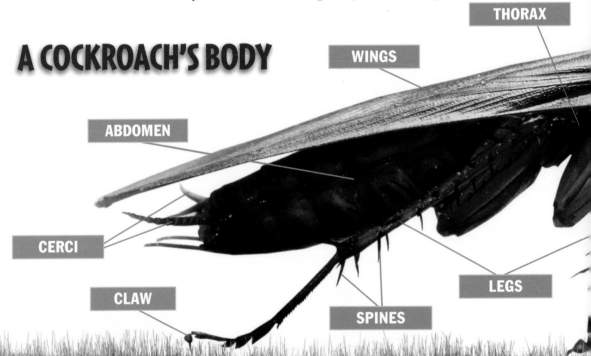

THORAX

WINGS

ABDOMEN

CERCI

CLAW

SPINES

LEGS

A cockroach's legs and feet do more than help it move around. They are important sensory **organs**. The legs and feet have hairs and **spines** that sense movement, vibrations, and more. A cockroach's leg joints can even sense sounds. And, the feet have taste buds! This helps a cockroach sense when it wanders over a yummy treat.

The abdomen is the rear of the cockroach's body. This **segment** is much larger than the head or the thorax. That is because it houses most of the roach's organs.

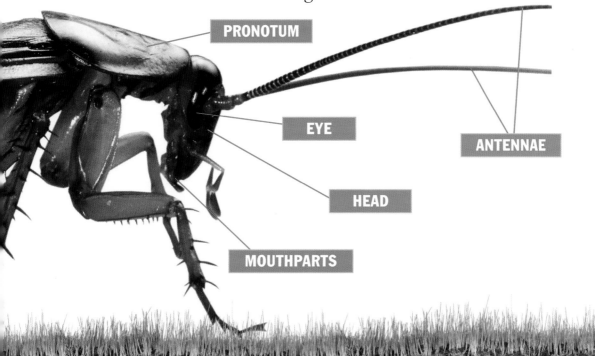

PRONOTUM

EYE

ANTENNAE

HEAD

MOUTHPARTS

The Inside Story

Inside a cockroach, important **organs** and body systems work together to keep its body moving. Its respiratory system is much different from a human's! A cockroach breathes through holes in its exoskeleton called spiracles. The spiracles are connected to tracheae, which help air travel around the bug's body.

Like many insects, a cockroach has an open circulatory system. That means blood flows freely throughout a cockroach's body, rather than through veins. Cockroach blood is called hemolymph. The cockroach's heart is a long tube. It keeps the hemolymph circulating from end to end.

A cockroach likes to snack on many gross things. After a meal, food travels through the **digestive** system. From the cockroach's mouthparts, food moves to its stomach, or crop. The crop stores food until it passes into the gizzard. There, tiny teeth mash the food into smaller pieces for digestion. Waste products leave the cockroach's body through the anus.

BUG BYTES

A cockroach can hold its breath for up to 40 minutes underwater. No wonder it is able to crawl up drainpipes!

A cockroach's body systems help it run fast. Most roaches are able to reach a speed of 50 body lengths per second! While running, some cockroaches spread their wings. This allows the air to lift them onto their hind legs.

Transformation

The cockroach's life cycle is called incomplete **metamorphosis**. This type of life cycle has three stages. These are egg, nymph, and adult. Most cockroaches take one and a half years to complete this cycle.

The life cycle begins after a male and female cockroach mate. Once the female's eggs are **fertilized**, she surrounds them with a hard substance. This forms a single egg case, or ootheca. The brown,

LIFE CYCLE OF A COCKROACH

EGG CASE

NYMPH

rounded bundle rests near the end of the female's abdomen. She keeps the egg case here while searching for a safe location to lay it.

A female cockroach may simply drop her egg case near a food source. Or, she may use a sticky substance to glue it onto a sheltered surface. This could be under a cabinet, in a nook, or in a small hole. Depending on her species, a female cockroach may keep her egg case within her abdomen. As a result, she gives birth to live young.

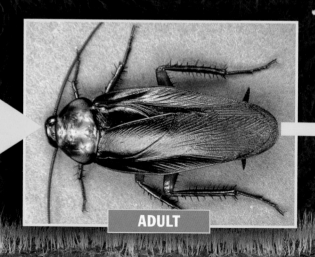

ADULT

Baby cockroaches begin to grow within their egg case. During this time, they hatch from their individual eggs. These little cockroaches are called nymphs.

Soon, the egg case breaks and the nymphs fall out. A nymph's exoskeleton is white and soft. But after it emerges, the exoskeleton quickly hardens and turns brown. The entire process takes several weeks from the time the eggs begin to develop. For example, an American cockroach leaves its egg case after six weeks.

The little roaches continue to grow. In fact, nymphs grow right out of their skin! This is called molting. Each time a nymph sheds its old skin, it reveals a new, bigger one. Molting takes place several times during the nymph stage.

When growth is complete, the nymph enters the adult stage. As an adult, a male cockroach seeks out a mate. He may flap his wings together to attract a female. A female cockroach that is ready to reproduce releases **pheromones** that lead a male to her. Soon, the life cycle begins all over again.

BUG BYTES

The average female cockroach produces about 130 eggs in her lifetime. The German cockroach can produce up to 400 eggs.

Immediately after molting, cockroaches are white. But, their exoskeletons will harden and darken within a few hours.

Roach Homes

Where are cockroaches found? Everywhere! Roaches live across the globe. Some have even been found at the North and South poles. Their adaptable diet and hardy bodies allow them to live in almost any climate.

Tropical cockroaches generally live on the damp forest floor among plant debris. Some species dwell in other dark places, such as caves.

Still, the cockroach's natural **habitat** is wet and warm. Therefore, huge numbers of them are found in tropical areas. In fact, most cockroach species live harmlessly in rain forests and other warm regions.

However, some cockroach species seek shelter in residential areas. They invade basements, kitchens, and bathrooms. Others hang around outside under decks, in piles of debris, and in yards.

Huge numbers of cockroaches also live in sewers. Sewers offer the perfect warm, wet surroundings that cockroaches love. They also contain plenty of the cockroach's favorite foods.

Large German cockroach populations can create unclean conditions. Exposure to their waste and spit can cause skin allergies and breathing problems.

A BAD REPUTATION

AMONG COCKROACHES, NONE IS AS TERRIBLE OF A PEST AS THE GERMAN COCKROACH. THIS SPECIES IS ALSO THE MOST COMMON COCKROACH PEST. IT IS FOUND WORLDWIDE WHEREVER HUMANS LIVE. IN FACT, THESE BUGS DEPEND ON HUMANS. THEY USE OUR WARM BUILDINGS AND EASY FOOD SOURCES TO SURVIVE.

THE GERMAN COCKROACH IS SOMETIMES CALLED THE CROTON BUG. THAT IS BECAUSE IT ONCE OCCUPIED THE CROTON WATER SEWER SYSTEM IN NEW YORK CITY, NEW YORK. DURING THE 1800S, THE ROACHES WERE FOUND IN HUGE NUMBERS THERE.

Favorite Foods

Yes, sewage is one of the cockroach's favorite foods. But cockroaches will eat anything. That includes dead plants and animals, animal waste, and garbage. This is why roaches are abundant in dirty areas such as sewers and dumpsters.

On the other hand, cockroaches can also be found in the cleanest places. That is because in addition to gross stuff, they also feast on the foods you like to eat.

Cockroaches love many foods including candy, baked goods, fish, nuts, and grease. If these kinds of

In tropical areas, some cockroaches obtain liquids from other insects. For example, lantern bugs provide cockroaches with a sugary liquid food called honeydew.

A cockroach can live for a month without food. However, it can only survive for a week without water.

foods are not available, roaches will move on to nonfood items. These include books, furniture, fabrics, wood, glue, and more.

In nature, cockroaches prefer rotted wood, decaying animals, and animal waste. They also include a wide variety of plants in their diet. This includes anything from garden plants to houseplants.

Beware!

Now you know that cockroaches eat just about anything they can get their mouths on. But do any creatures eat cockroaches? Frogs, lizards, and snakes are just a few of the roach's many natural predators. Birds and mice enjoy the crunch of a good cockroach. Spiders and insects also make cockroaches a part of their diet. Even tiny ants nibble on dead or wounded cockroaches.

CERCI

A cockroach's greatest enemies are centipedes and wasps. House centipedes love to eat cockroach nymphs. They feast away on this easy meal. Some wasp species use cockroach egg cases to lay their own eggs. The wasp babies eat the unhatched cockroach eggs. So, humans sometimes use these wasps to control the roach population.

Yet, cockroaches have well-developed survival defenses. For instance, two feelers called cerci stick out from the cockroach's rear end. They detect changes in the cockroach's surroundings. These include vibrations and changes in air movement. Such signals tell the cockroach to run!

Instead of running away, some cockroach species play dead. Some even make themselves smell dead! Others can project acidic **fluids** from their abdomen.

Cockroaches are fast runners. But they are no match for wolf spiders. These spiders are skilled hunters that run down their prey.

Roaches and You

Obviously, a large percentage of people really dislike cockroaches. Finding them in a tub, a sink, or a shower is an unwelcome surprise.

Once cockroaches have found a way into your house, you can bet they won't want to leave. Instead, they will want to start a family! And cockroaches reproduce very quickly. When roaches move inside and multiply, they become pests.

In addition to being annoying, the presence of cockroaches can be unhealthy. When cockroaches eat dead and decaying plants and animals, they also eat **germs**.

Cockroaches also pick up germs when they crawl out of drainpipes. Then, these roaches spread germs from their feet to the surfaces they walk on. At night, they come out and walk across your food and countertops. They also leave behind trails of their waste. Finding these remains on your food isn't just gross. These conditions can lead to the spread of disease.

BUG BYTES

Twelve cockroaches can survive for a week on just the glue of one postage stamp!

Roaches can survive in almost all types of conditions. However, dirt and debris make life much easier for them!

There are many good reasons to keep cockroaches outdoors in their natural **habitat**. Luckily, steps can be taken to discourage them from coming inside.

Cockroaches need water to survive. So houses, restaurants, and other structures should be controlled for dampness. They should also be free of obvious entryways for cockroaches.

Inside, keeping clean can help discourage these insects from settling in for a feast. Make sure to wash dirty dishes right away. And, you should always wrap and put away foods.

Despite the gross facts about cockroaches, there are still people who like these insects. For example, the giant rhinoceros cockroach

Giant rhinoceros cockroaches can grow as long as 3 inches (8 cm). They can weigh up to 1.2 ounces (34 g). These bugs are also known to live as long as 10 years.

is considered a great pet! This species is gentle and lives cleanly. It also eats healthy foods, such as leaves. Some cockroach owners even claim their cockroach pets like to cuddle.

How do you feel about cockroaches now? You still may not want one for a pet. That's okay. But hopefully you won't be freaked out the next time you see one!

Glossary

digest - to break down food into substances small enough for the body to absorb. The process of digesting food is called digestion. This is carried out by the digestive system.

entomologist - a scientist who studies insects.

fertilize - to make fertile. Something that is fertile is capable of growing or developing.

fluid - a substance, such as a liquid or a gas, that flows or takes the shape of its container.

germ - a harmful organism, such as bacteria, that causes disease.

habitat - a place where a living thing is naturally found.

metamorphosis - the process of change in the form and habits of some animals during development from an immature stage to an adult stage.

organ - a part of an animal or a plant that is composed of several kinds of tissues and that performs a specific function. The heart, liver, gallbladder, and intestines are organs of an animal.

pheromone - a chemical substance produced by an animal. It serves as a signal to other individuals of the same species to engage in some kind of behavior.

segment - any of the parts into which a thing is divided or naturally separates.

spine - a stiff, pointed projection on an animal.

suborder - a group of related organisms ranking between an order and a family.

superfamily - a group of related organisms ranking below an order and containing more than one family.

How Do You Say That?

antennae - an-TEH-nee
Blattaria - bla-TAYR-ee-uh
cerci - SUHR-seye
chitin - KEYE-tuhn
Dictyoptera - dihk-tee-AHP-tuh-ruh
hemolymph - HEE-muh-lihmf
maxillae - mak-SIH-lee
metamorphosis - meh-tuh-MAWR-fuh-suhs
nymph - NIHMF
ocelli - oh-SEH-leye
ootheca - oh-uh-THEE-kuh
pronotum - proh-NOH-tuhm
tracheae - TRAY-kee-ee

Web Sites

To learn more about cockroaches, visit ABDO Publishing Company on the World Wide Web at **www.abdopublishing.com**. Web sites about cockroaches are featured on our Book Links page. These links are routinely monitored and updated to provide the most current information available.

Index